Improvising Lead Guitar

Intermediate Level

by

Tony Skinner

A CIP record for this publication is available from the British Library.

ISBN: 1-898466-37-8

Published in Great Britain by

Registry Mews, 11-13 Wilton Road, Bexhill, Sussex, TN40 1HY, United Kingdom

Typesetting by

Take Note Publishing Ltd., Lingfield, Surrey

Printed in Great Britain

Contents

Page

CD running order

Introduction

The purpose of this book is to help you further improve your lead guitar improvisation skills, by developing your ability to create solos in a wide range of musical styles and keys. An extensive range of scales and arpeggios is shown, together with essential practical information about how and where to use them.

The accompanying CD provides a full band backing track for all the chord sequences shown within this book. By playing along with the CD you'll be able to hear exactly how your lead guitar improvisation sounds in a real band setting.

get tuned

Before you start playing you'll need to get your guitar in tune. The CD tuning guide (Track I) gives you the pitch of each string starting with the low E string. Although you could use an electronic tuner to help you check the notes, it's a good idea to use the CD tuning guide as often as you can as this will help you develop your sense of pitch.

get graded

This book is structured in line with the Registry Of Guitar Tutors' electric guitar examination syllabus – which is validated by London College of Music Examinations (one of the world's longest established music examination boards) and certificated by Thames Valley University.

All the scales, arpeggios and chord progressions shown have been chosen to reflect the exact requirements of the *Lead Guitar* sections of the Grade Three, Four and Five RGT examinations.

The book therefore provides an ideal study aid for those preparing to take any of the Registry of Guitar Tutors' electric guitar examinations from Grade Three to Five. However, the book is designed so that it can be used by all guitar players – whether intending to take an examination or not.

If you wish to obtain a FREE electric guitar examination information pack, contact:

Registry of Guitar Tutors
Registry Mews
11-13 Wilton Road
Bexhill
Sussex
TN40 1HY
United Kingdom

www.RegistryOfGuitarTutors.com
01424 22 22 22

How to improvise

First of all, what does 'improvisation' mean? Well, it's not simply about playing scales up and down. Neither is it just about instantly creating melodies without reference to scales. The truth lies somewhere between the two, and the ideal mix needs the addition of a few other ingredients as well – such as the use of phrasing, stylistic interpretation and specialist techniques. So whilst guitar improvising might typically be defined as *making up a lead solo on the spot*, in reality there's a lot of background work and knowledge underpinning this.

know your scales

> ***"Learn your scales thoroughly... up, down and inside out!"***

To solo over any chord sequence you'll need to know the correct scale to use. This will define the choice of notes that will fit with the backing chords of the key. Before you start any improvisation you should play through the appropriate scale several times until you are totally familiar with it. Remember, it's the scale that determines which notes will fit with the backing chords. You should know it so well that you can relax whilst playing it, and be free to focus your attention on using the scale creatively to make an interesting solo. The most useful scales for the intermediate level player are displayed later on in this book.

using arpeggios

> ***"Try arpeggios now and again... they'll always fit in."***

An arpeggio is simply the notes of a chord played sequentially. Because each arpeggio contains exactly the same notes as its related chord you can never play a wrong note if you use an arpeggio correctly.

Using arpeggios for lead playing is harder than just using a normal key scale, because you need to change the arpeggio every time the backing chord changes. In most pop and rock styles, guitarists rarely use arpeggios throughout a whole solo – instead arpeggios are used only occasionally to add colour, whilst the normal key scale is used for the majority of the solo.

Practising arpeggios is very useful, as this helps you identify the notes contained within each chord. You can use this knowledge to target certain chord tones – even whilst using basic scales.

develop phrasing

> ***"Leave gaps... there's no need to play continuously."***

Once you're sure that you know your way around the scales, you can start to improvise some lead work over one of the backing chord sequences that are shown in this book (and featured on the CD).

- Try to invent memorable phrases rather than a continuous flurry of notes, and don't be scared to leave gaps.
- You don't need to play all the notes of the scale, nor in any particular order (and certainly not in the set scale order). Once you have learnt the scale, the aim is to use it in a melodically inventive and creative way.
- You can avoid sounding too scale-like by singing, or thinking up phrases in your mind, and then trying to reproduce them on the guitar. Even if, at first, you are unable to reproduce the exact melody of what you had in mind, you should at least be able to reproduce the rhythm of your phrase reasonably accurately.
- Using your imagination to develop phrases will create a more natural feel to your lead playing than allowing your fingers to lead the way.

trust your ear

"You can avoid wrong notes... just rely on the scale."

As long as you've chosen the correct scale, there's no need to worry about playing wrong notes; all the notes in the scale WILL fit over the chords – although some will sound more harmonically resolved than others over particular chords. Let your ears guide you as to which ones sound best. If you hit a note that sounds too unresolved for your liking, simply move smoothly and deliberately onto the next note (above or below) in the scale and this will always sound fine. Play some notes that are NOT in the scale against the backing track and you'll soon hear the difference – the ones outside the scale will clash with the chords and sound completely wrong.

Plectrum technique

If you hold the plectrum the wrong way it can slow down your playing for years to come. The best method is to grip the plectrum between the thumb and index finger. Position the plectrum so that its point is about half a centimetre beyond the fingertip. If you let too much poke through it may snag on the string; too little and you may miss the string totally. Also, be careful how you grip the plectrum. If you use too much pressure your hand muscles will tighten and so reduce your fluency, but don't hold it so loosely that you keep dropping it.

Registry RGT Registry of Guitar Tutors

how to pick

In order that your wrist can move freely, hold the plectrum so that it is in-line with your fingernail. Avoid holding it at right angles to your index finger as this will cause your wrist to lock. To gain speed and fluency, it's essential that the picking movement comes from the wrist, NOT from the elbow. Unless you're trying to produce a particular effect, you should always alternate down and up plectrum strokes. This will enable you to achieve much greater speed and fluency than if you only use the pick in one direction.

Stages to improvising

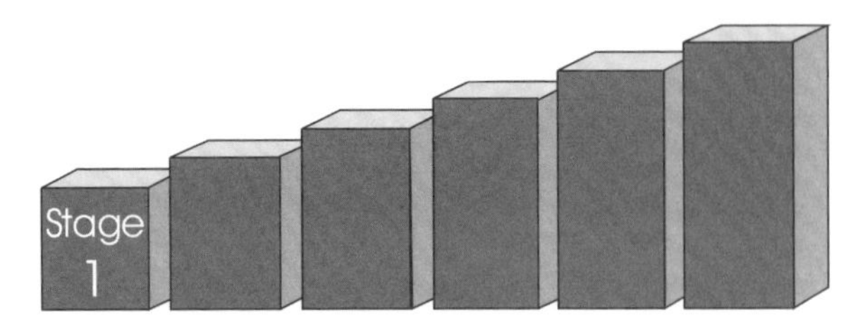

get in key

> ***"Choose the right scale before you start to play."***

Before you begin to play any lead you'll need to identify the key of the song. Since nearly all songs begin with the tonic (i.e. home key) chord, the easiest method is to check the first chord of the song. For example:

- if the first chord is A minor, you can be pretty certain that the song is in the key of A minor, and so your lead playing should normally come from either the A natural minor or A pentatonic minor scale.
  The pentatonic minor is simply a shortened five note version of the natural minor scale – so in practice the two are interchangeable. Because the natural minor has more notes it can be more melodic in character. The pentatonic minor scale has a harder edged sound which is very suited to rock styles. The harmonic minor scale is best used only in minor key sequences when the chord built on the fifth degree of the scale is a dominant 7th – e.g. when E7 (rather than Em) occurs in the key A minor.

- if the first chord is D major then you should use either the D major or D pentatonic major scale.
  The pentatonic major is simply a shortened five note version of the major scale – so in practice the two scales are interchangeable. The major scale is intrinsically the more melodic of the two. The pentatonic major scale has a more open sound and is often used in country and rock styles.

- the blues scale is designed to be used over bluesy chord sequences, which normally start with a dominant 7th chord. So if a song begins with an A7 chord, then A blues scale might be a good choice of scale to use.
  Avoid starting, or lingering, on the ♭5 note within this scale as it can sound slightly dissonant. It is intended as a 'passing note' – so just pass through it on the way to another note.

It doesn't matter how fast and flashy your lead playing is; if you use the wrong scale you're certain to hit notes that will clash with the backing chords.

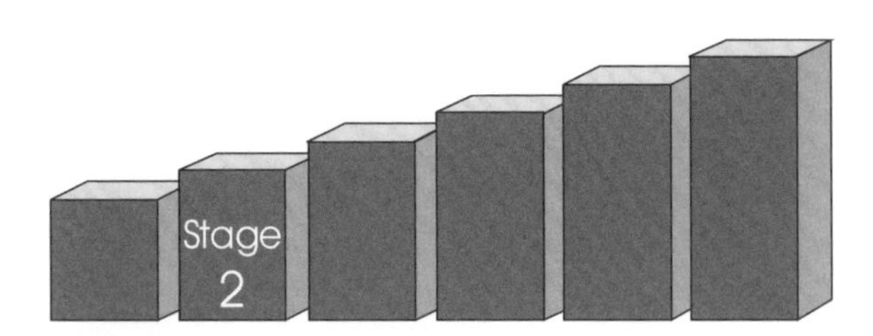

try the scale

> ***"Practise the scale and experiment with rhythms."***

Once you're sure which scale to use, start by simply playing the scale up and down over the backing track so that you can begin to hear the overall sound and tonality of the key. Then, rather than playing the scale in straight time, experiment by playing some notes quickly whilst allowing others to ring on. You'll notice that this sounds far more musical and inventive than the straight scale, even though you're still playing the same notes in the same order. Once you're familiar with the sound of the scale you should try to use it in a melodically inventive and creative way. The scale only defines the choice of notes that will fit with the chords in the key. Simply playing the scale up and down is not enough to make a good solo.

Stage
3

use repetition

> *"Repeat phrases to give your solo structure"*

By repeating a series of notes from the scale you will begin to establish licks or phrases that will become memorable to the listener. Once you have a phrase that you like, try and vary it slightly when you repeat it – that way it will sound fresh, whilst still giving the listener something recognisable to latch onto. By repeating clusters of notes you can start to develop melodic phrasing and structure.

Try and leave gaps between your phrases, so that the music has space to breathe. Remember that it's not always necessary to play turbo speed licks to make a great guitar solo – the choice of just a few carefully selected and well-executed notes can often have far greater emotional impact. Sometimes the saying 'less is more' gives the best clue to establishing the right *feel* for a piece of music.

Occasionally though, some music calls for an insistent and continuous driving rhythm. It all depends on the type of music. It's up to you to listen carefully to the accompaniment and use your own musical judgement to decide upon the best form of stylistic interpretation.

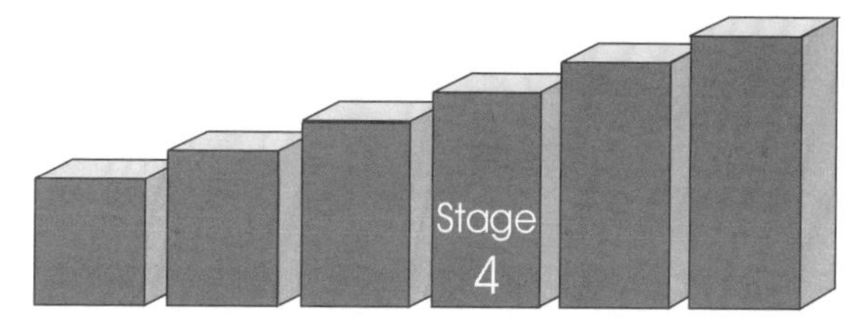

now phrase it

> *"Create memorable phrases and allow the music space to breathe."*

Experiment with the scales and try to improvise your own solos over the backing tracks. But do remember, scales simply set the choice of notes that will fit in any key. It's up to you to create melodically and rhythmically interesting phrases from the scale.

- Experiment by playing phrases of different lengths and listen carefully to your playing to hear which ones best suit the musical style.

- Avoid making your phrasing sound too predictable by not always starting phrases on the first beat of the bar. Instead, try playing a few 'lead-in' notes before the start of the first bar.

- Ensure that you use a wide variety of note lengths. Play some notes quickly and allow others to ring on.

The important thing is to let your ears and intuition, rather than your fingers, guide you. For inspiration, spend some time listening to recordings by well known musicians (not just guitarists) in a wide range of musical styles.

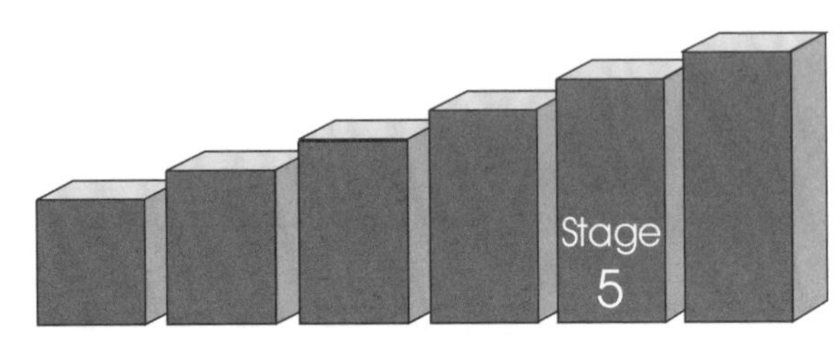

target arpeggios

> ***"Arpeggios are a good way of breaking away from monotonous scale playing."***

You might be surprised to learn that most basic chords (and therefore arpeggios) contain only three or four notes. Taking an example of a G major barré chord: although you strum six strings, the pitch of the notes (from the bass string upwards) are G D G B D G. In other words, there are just three different notes within the chord – some notes are repeated just to make the chord sound fuller. If you play the three notes (G B D) one after another you end up with an arpeggio. You can then swap these notes around, or repeat some, to make up a more interesting musical phrase – just as you would when improvising with a scale.

The really handy thing is, because the arpeggio contains exactly the same notes as the chord, whatever notes you play from the arpeggio will always fit well with the chord. The downside of this is that, unlike a scale, you need to change the arpeggio every time the chord changes. However, you don't need to play a solo consisting entirely of arpeggios – instead use them sparingly to add structure and solidity to your improvisation.

Practising arpeggios should also help you learn the names of the notes contained within each chord. Use this knowledge to target chord tones (notes from the chord being played) whilst improvising with the key scale. For example, whilst using the G major scale in a sequence in G major, over the chord of G you could start or end your phrase with either a G, B or D note (i.e. one of the notes from the G arpeggio/chord). Then if the chord changes to A minor, you could target either A, C or E from the G major scale (i.e. one of the notes from the A minor arpeggio/chord).

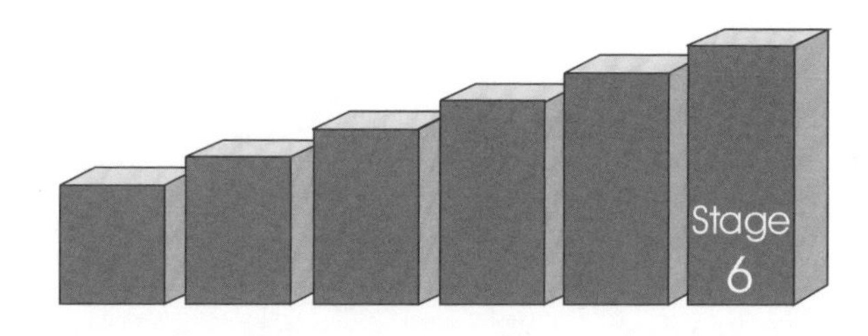

bend it shake it

> *"To turn your improvisation into a real guitar solo you'll need to use some specialist guitar techniques."*

Try bending some notes up in pitch, or get a vibrato effect by wavering the pitch of some notes slightly. You could also slur some notes by, for instance, hammering some notes on, rather than picking every note with the plectrum.

Using bends and other specialist techniques gives improvisation a real guitar feel, and can add character and style to a solo that might otherwise be a little dull. Explanations of these techniques are given below and overleaf (under the heading Specialist Techniques).

String Bending Technique

To physically bend a note all you have to do is fret it normally and then push it skywards with your fingers. If you're executing the bend with the third or fourth finger, it's important that you use the remaining fingers as well, on the same string, to give you added strength when bending. Ignoring this advice will either mean that your bends won't go high enough to be in tune, or if they do, then you'll possibly cause yourself a finger injury. Don't try string bending using just one finger – it can be dangerous!

You should push the string upwards until it reaches the pitch of the following note in the scale. It's a good idea to practise fretting the higher note first, and then singing that note aloud, whilst bending the note into tune. The essential thing is to listen as you bend. Beware – not much sounds worse than badly out of tune string bending.

In theory, you can bend any note in any scale providing that it reaches another note in that scale. In practice, it's best, at first, to restrict yourself to just a few notes that will generally work in most situations. The easiest (whole-tone) bends for each scale are given after each chord sequence.

Practise string bending in different keys. This is important as the amount of pressure that will be needed will vary depending upon the fingerboard position. For instance, bending a note on the third fret of the G string will require more strength than bending on the seventh fret of the same string.

Specialist techniques

Slurs

Slurring can make your playing both awesomely fast and super smooth. It comprises two main techniques: *hammering-on* and *pulling-off*. Each technique allows you to sound two or more notes for each pick of a string.

To hammer-on a note:

instead of picking the string again as normal, rapidly hammer the tip of your fretting finger onto the note that you want. Providing you hammer-on right next to the fretwire, the note should come out as clearly as if you had picked it normally. If it doesn't, then you're probably not hammering hard enough!

To pull-off a note:

first fret a note and pick the string, then pull your fretting finger lightly *downwards* until it plucks the string and the lower note is sounded. If the lower note is fretted (rather than an open string) then you need to have another finger in position fretting this note before executing the pull-off, and you should also ensure that it is held with firm pressure so that the pulling finger doesn't cause it to move and alter pitch.

Multi-slurs

once you've mastered the basic techniques you can try slurring more than one note. For example, play the note of A, then hammer-on B and then hammer-on C – or play these three notes in reverse using pull-offs. You can combine hammer-ons and pull-offs to make a *trill* by repeatedly slurring between two notes. There are literally hundreds of possible combinations and the only limit is your imagination. The trick is to experiment with as many different slurs as possible.

Slides

You can slide quickly to a note from a few frets below (or even above) and as long as you don't linger on the initial note, it doesn't matter where you start from. Alternatively, you can play and hold a lower note in a scale before sliding slowly to a higher note in that scale. (You can allow any intervening passing notes to sound and create a colourful chromatic effect.) Slides can be a highly effective musical technique – as long as they're not overused.

When sliding up the fingerboard make sure that you move the whole hand including the thumb, rather than just the fretting finger. If you find this difficult, commercially available string lubricants will help make the strings and fingerboard slippery.

Vibrato

By repeatedly varying the pitch of a note very slightly you can achieve an effect known as *vibrato*. This effect is used by many musicians to add sustain and tone to their playing.

On a steel strung-guitar, you can get a vibrato effect by repeatedly waggling the tip of your fretting finger vertically up and down very slightly whilst holding a note. On a nylon-strung guitar, you can get a similar effect by moving the finger horizontally.

If you are fretting the note with your first finger then you can use 'wrist vibrato' – where the pitch of the note is altered by the rotation of the wrist, whilst the first finger holds down the note.

String bends

You can string bend (i.e. change the pitch of a note without altering string or fingerboard position) by fretting a note and pushing the string upwards whilst you pick it. String bends are a great way of adding expression to your playing. Nearly all rock and blues guitarists use string bending as an integral part of their technique, and as a way of expressing emotion through their playing.

How to bend

When string bending with the third finger always keep your first and second fingers on the string to give support and control to the bending finger. Pivot from the elbow, to use the strength of the whole forearm when string bending. This way you'll avoid any risk of injuring your finger.

Don't be scared to position your thumb over the top of the fingerboard if you find that this gives you extra leverage.

How high should I go?

You should bend a note until it reaches the pitch of the next note in the scale. Be careful to pitch the note exactly in tune when bending. One way to practise this is to fret a note and sing the pitch produced; then using this as a target note play a note two frets lower and slowly bend it upwards until it becomes in tune with your singing.

Top ten bends

1. *Rising bend.* Repeatedly pick the string whilst bending it up very slowly. This is a good first bend to learn as you can hear the note gradually bend into tune.
2. *Choke bend.* Bend the note, then quickly choke the sound by letting the picking hand touch the strings. This gives the staccato sound much favoured by blues players. Because it's so short, the pitch is less exposed – so this is one of the easiest bends to use at first without worrying too much about tuning.
3. *Teasing bend.* Use several very small bends before fully bending the note into tune. This creates a very communicative, almost speaking effect.
4. *Hold bend.* Bend the note slowly until it's in tune – then just hold it there. This is a favourite technique of guitarists who prefer a long sustained tone. Although it's the easiest sounding bend don't be surprised if, at first, you find it tricky to keep the note exactly in tune. It may take some practice to perfect this one!
5. *Release bend.* Bend the note up without picking it – then pick it and slowly release it. This is a way of making a note go down in pitch. Don't try this one until you've perfected the hold bend or you'll be starting from an out of tune note.
6. *Up down bend.* Bend the note up and, without re-picking it, let it down again. That way you get two notes for the price of one!
7. *Double bend.* Bend the note up, let it down, and then bend it up again – but only pick the string the first time.
8. *Waver bend.* Bend the note up and then repeatedly lower and raise it very slightly – so that you are adding vibrato to the bent note.
9. *Unison bend.* Whilst bending to a note, fret and play the same note on the next string. For example, simultaneously play D fretted on the 1st string, and C (being bent up to D) on the 2nd string. It also sounds good to alternate between the two strings.
10. *Harmony bend.* Bend a note whilst playing and holding a different note higher in the scale.

Guitarograph

All the scales and arpeggios within this book are illustrated using the Registry Of Guitar Tutors' unique Guitarograph system. This incorporates tablature, standard musical notation, interval formula and fingerboard information all in one diagram. As the guitarograph illustrates the same information in this unique combination of four different systems there should be no doubt how to play any scale or arpeggio.

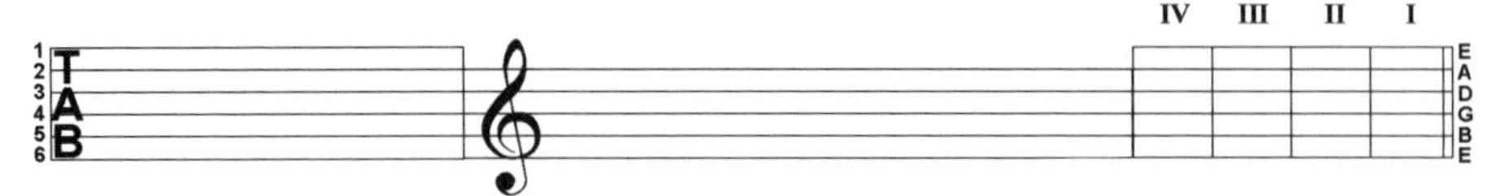

tablature

The tablature is shown on the left of the guitarograph, with horizontal lines representing the strings (with the high E string being string 1), and the numbers on the string lines referring to the frets.

musical notation

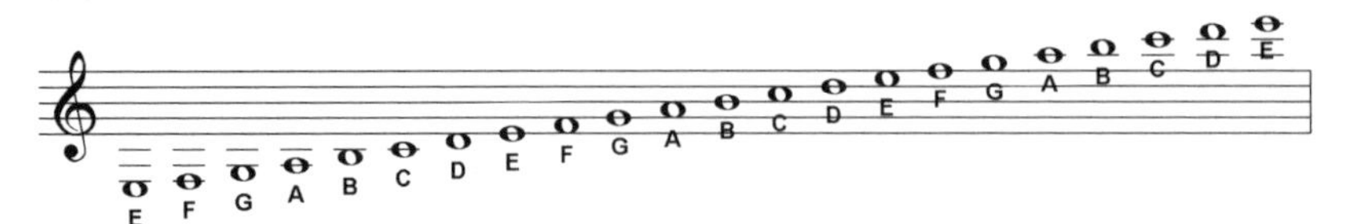

The middle section of each guitarograph illustrates the scale in standard musical notation.

fingerboard diagram

The fingerboard diagram is on the right of the guitarograph with horizontal lines representing the strings. Vertical lines represent the frets; with fret numbers shown in Roman numerals. Numbers on the horizontal lines show the recommended fingering.

interval formula

C	D	E	F	G	A	B	C
1	2	3	4	5	6	7	8

Above each guitarograph is an interval formula listing the pitch of the notes together with their interval numbers (shown in comparison to the major scale with the same starting pitch). The interval formulae are designed to help you identify the differences in construction between the various scales and arpeggios and to help you learn the names of the notes you are playing. A thorough knowledge of the notes on the fingerboard provides a sound foundation for developing your guitar playing. Spending time memorising the notes of each scale and arpeggio, and where they occur on the fingerboard, will prove a worthwhile investment.

Fingering options

All the scales and arpeggios within this book are 'transpositional' – i.e. they use moveable patterns that you can shift up or down the fingerboard to any key. For example, the A natural minor scale (shown on page 18), which starts on A at the fifth fret of the E string, can be transposed to C natural minor by simply starting the same pattern on C (at the eighth fret of the same string).

The fingerings which have been chosen are those which are most likely to be effective for the widest range of players at this level. However, alternative fingerings and fingerboard positions could be used and you should feel free to explore any systematic fingerings which produce a good musical result.

using all four

> *"Using your little finger can make things easier in the long run."*

In general you should use a 'one finger per fret' technique. This involves using all four fingers of the fretting hand when necessary. There is often a great temptation not to use the fourth finger as it feels weaker than the others. However, this means you will be operating at only 75% of your potential. Having said that, you may discover that several very famous and respected players of the past often used only three fingers. However this doesn't mean that this is going to be the easiest, or the most effective, method for you – particularly if you ever want to venture into the more technically demanding styles of guitar playing.

- By not incorporating the fourth finger into your technique it will take you many more hours of practice to play the same complex riff than someone who is using all their fingers.
- Once you do start using the little finger regularly it will develop strength and eventually you will feel as confident in using it as you do your other fingers.

at the edge

> *"To avoid fretbuzz press close to the fretwire."*

With all scales, you should stretch your fingers out so that you can press with your fingertips at the very edge of the frets – right next to the fretwire. This way you will not only avoid fretbuzz, but also you won't have to press too hard.

- Before you play, get in position and have you fingers ready in a 'hovering' position covering all the frets you are about to use. It may seem somewhat of a stretch at first, but do persevere – it really does get easier with practice.
- If you press in the middle of the fret (away from the fretwire) you will find that it's much harder to achieve clarity.
- When playing two or more notes on the same string keep the lower fingers on – in case you go back to those notes.
- To get a clear sound, press with the tips (rather than the pads) of your fingers.

Start playing

The most useful scales and arpeggios for Intermediate Level improvisation are illustrated on the following pages. These are also the same scales and arpeggios required for the Registry Of Guitar Tutors electric guitar examinations – Grades 3 to 5.

If you find these scales very difficult to play you should review the previous books in this series (Improvising Lead Guitar – 'Total Beginner', 'Beginner Plus', and 'Improver Level') before proceeding.

listen first

On the following pages you'll find the chord sequences which are featured on the accompanying CD. Listen to at least one sequence of each backing track before beginning to improvise – that way you will be able to get a good feel for the musical style and structure of the sequence.

playing levels

Below each sequence you'll find a scale which you can use to improvise your solo over the backing track. So that you learn in a progressive and structured way, the suggested scale will vary according to playing level.

It is recommended that you play along with the backing tracks several times using the Grade Three level suggestions before progressing through the higher grade levels.

Grade 3 performance level:

- At this level you should concentrate on using only one fingerboard position for each scale.
- Once you're fully familiar with the scale, you can also try using some notes from an arpeggio over one of the chords – particularly where a chord stays the same for two bars. At this level, not too much arpeggio use should be attempted as it may interfere with your concentration on using the key scale to develop phrases.
- You should try and incorporate some basic use of specialist techniques (bends, slurs, vibrato etc.) as these will enhance the performance. The easiest string bending opportunities are given with each scale.

Grade 4 performance level:

- At this level you should try and use two fingerboard positions for each scale. You should be able to develop a wider range of phrases by moving between the two scale positions.
- Specialist techniques, and any arpeggio use, should be a little more confident and widespread than at Grade 3 level. And, depending upon the scale, you might be able to use a wider range of string bends.

Grade 5 performance level:

- At this level you should try and use up to five fingerboard positions for each scale. Try and develop fluency in moving between the different scale positions by thinking up phrases that start in one position and end in another. This can help make your playing far less repetitive than it might be if you played in just one position.
- You should be aiming to develop a good level of control over a variety of string bends and vibrato, and to be fairly at ease with incorporating notes from arpeggios into your soloing.

CD track 2 – Soul Rock

| 4/4 B♭ | Gm | B♭ | Gm | Cm | Cm | F | F ||

Grade 3 level performance	
Suggested scale:	B♭ pentatonic major – 2 octaves, 1 position
Best bends:	Upper octave – 2nd(C) to 3rd(D), 5th(F) to 6th(G)

Grade 4 level performance	
Suggested scale:	B♭ pentatonic major – 2 octaves, 2 positions

Grade 5 level performance	
Suggested scale:	B♭ pentatonic major – 2 octaves, 3 positions

B♭ pentatonic major scale – 2 octaves (3 fingerboard positions)

B♭	C	D	F	G	B♭
1	2	3	5	6	8

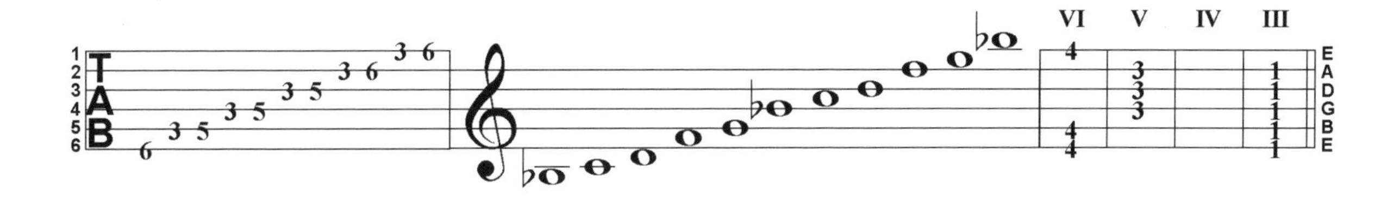

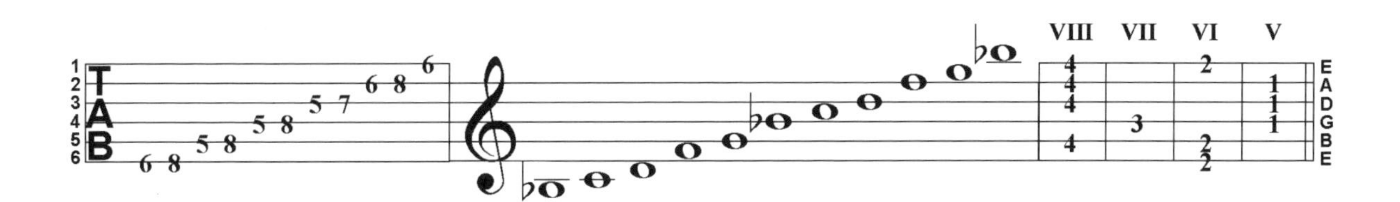

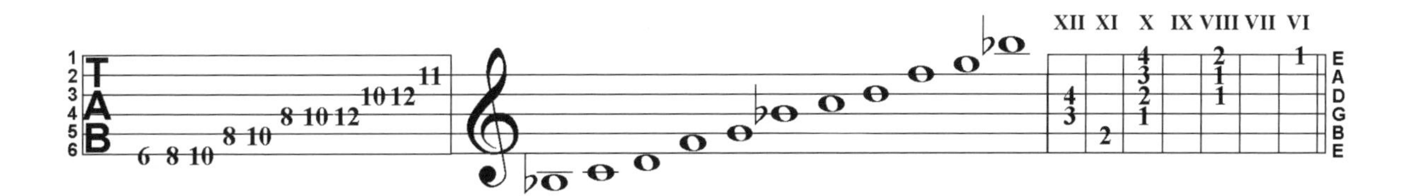

CD track 3 – Classic Rock

| 4/4 Am | Dm | G | Am | Dm | Dm | F | G ||

Grade 3 level performance	
Suggested scale:	A pentatonic minor or A natural minor – 2 octaves, 1 position
Best bends:	Upper octave – 4th(D) to 5th(E), ♭7th(G) to octave(A)

Grade 4 level performance	
Suggested scale:	A natural minor – 2 octaves, 2 positions
Best bends:	2nd position, upper octave – ♭3rd(C) to 4th(D)

Grade 5 level performance	
Suggested scale:	A pentatonic minor – 1 octave, 5 positions

A pentatonic minor scale – 2 octaves

A	C	D	E	G	A
1	♭3	4	5	♭7	8

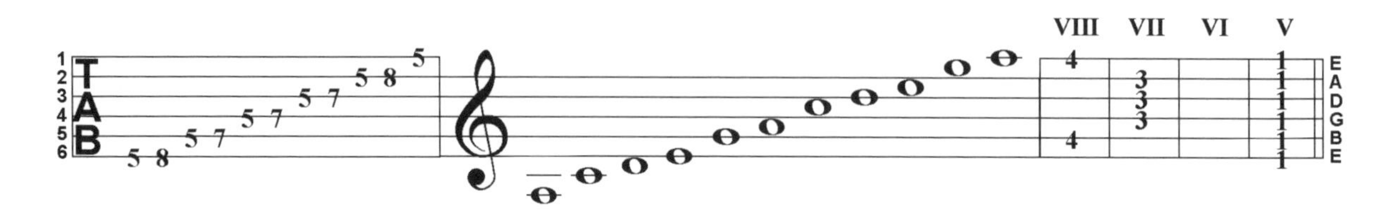

A natural minor scale – 2 octaves (2 fingerboard positions)

A	B	C	D	E	F	G	A
1	2	♭3	4	5	♭6	♭7	8

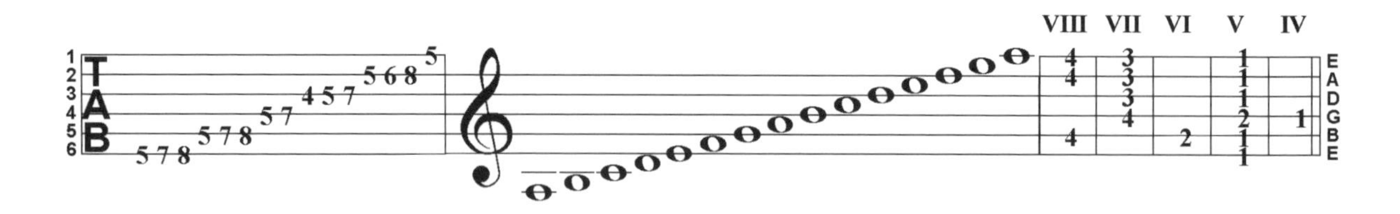

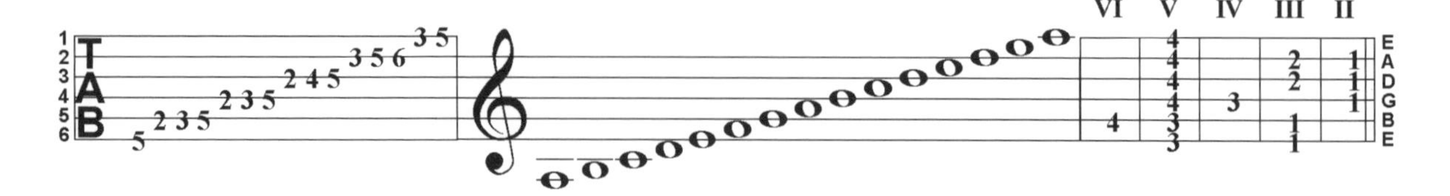

A pentatonic minor scale – 1 octave (5 fingerboard positions)

A C D E G A

1 ♭3 4 5 ♭7 8

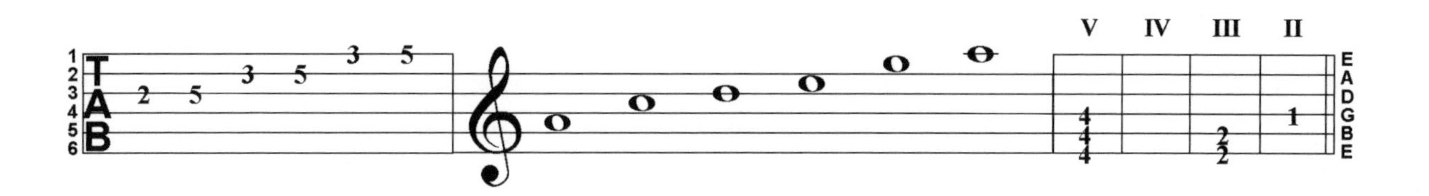

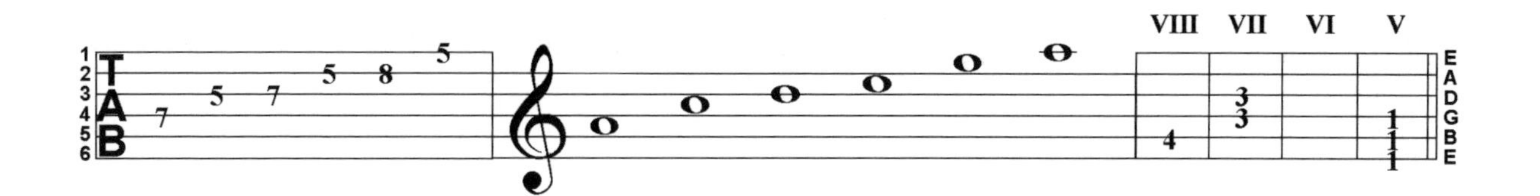

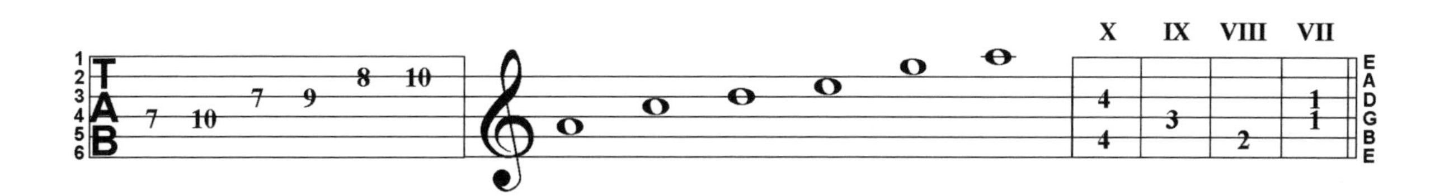

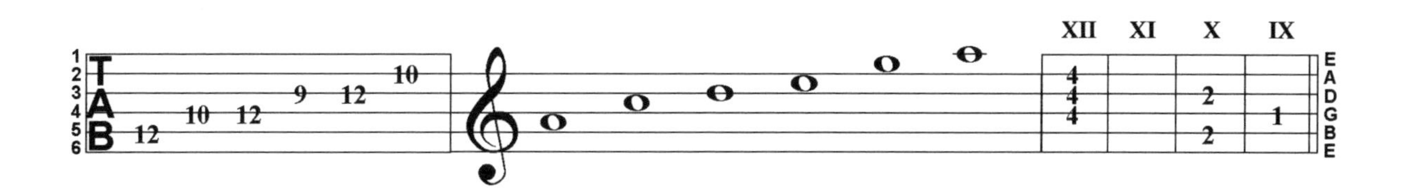

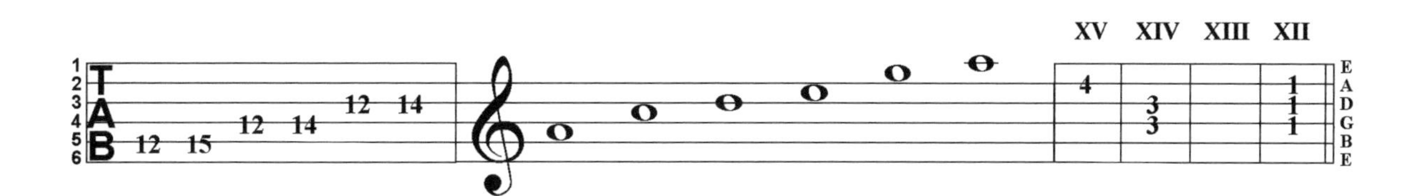

CD track 4 – Melodic Rock

| 4/4 ‖: Cm | B♭. A♭. | B♭ | B♭ :‖ Fm | Fm | A♭ | B♭ ‖

Grade 3 level performance	
Suggested scale:	C pentatonic minor or C natural minor – 2 octaves, 1 position
Best bends:	Upper octave – 4th(F) to 5th(G), ♭7th(B♭) to octave(C)

Grade 4 level performance	
Suggested scale:	C natural minor – 2 octaves, 2 positions
Best bends:	2nd shape, upper octave – ♭3rd(E♭) to 4th(F)

Grade 5 level performance	
Suggested scale:	C pentatonic minor – 1 octave, 5 positions

To learn the C pentatonic minor and C natural minor scales refer to the scale shapes shown on pages 18 and 19. These can be transposed to C minor by playing three frets higher than illustrated.

CD track 5 – Rock Ballad

| 4/4 Gm | F | Cm | Dm | E♭ | E♭ | Dm.Cm. | F ||

Grade 3 level performance	
Suggested scale:	G pentatonic minor or G natural minor – 2 octaves, 1 position
Best bends:	Upper octave – 4th(C) to 5th(D), ♭7th(F) to octave(G)

Grade 4 level performance	
Suggested scale:	G natural minor – 2 octaves, 2 positions
Best bends:	2nd shape, upper octave – ♭3rd(B♭) to 4th(C)

Grade 5 level performance	
Suggested scale:	G pentatonic minor – 1 octave, 5 positions

To learn the G pentatonic minor and G natural minor scales refer to the scale shapes shown on pages 18 and 19. These can be transposed to G minor by starting each shape on G rather than an A. (Some of the scale shapes can be played using open strings or transposed an octave higher.)

CD track 6 – Melodic Ballad

♫ = ♩♪ (3)

| 3/4 E | Emaj7 | A | Amaj7 | F♯m | F♯m7 | B | B7 ||

Grade 3 level performance	
Suggested scale:	E major – 2 octaves, 1 position

Grade 4 level performance	
Suggested scale:	E major – 2 octaves, 2 positions
Best bends:	Upper octaves – 2nd(F#) to 3rd(G#), 4th(A) to 5th(B), 5th(B) to 6th(C#), 6th(C#) to 7th(D#)

Grade 5 level performance	
Suggested scale:	E major – 1 octave, 3 positions

E major scale – 2 octaves (2 fingerboard positions)

E	F#	G#	A	B	C#	D#	E
1	2	3	4	5	6	7	8

E major scale – 1 octave (3 fingerboard positions)

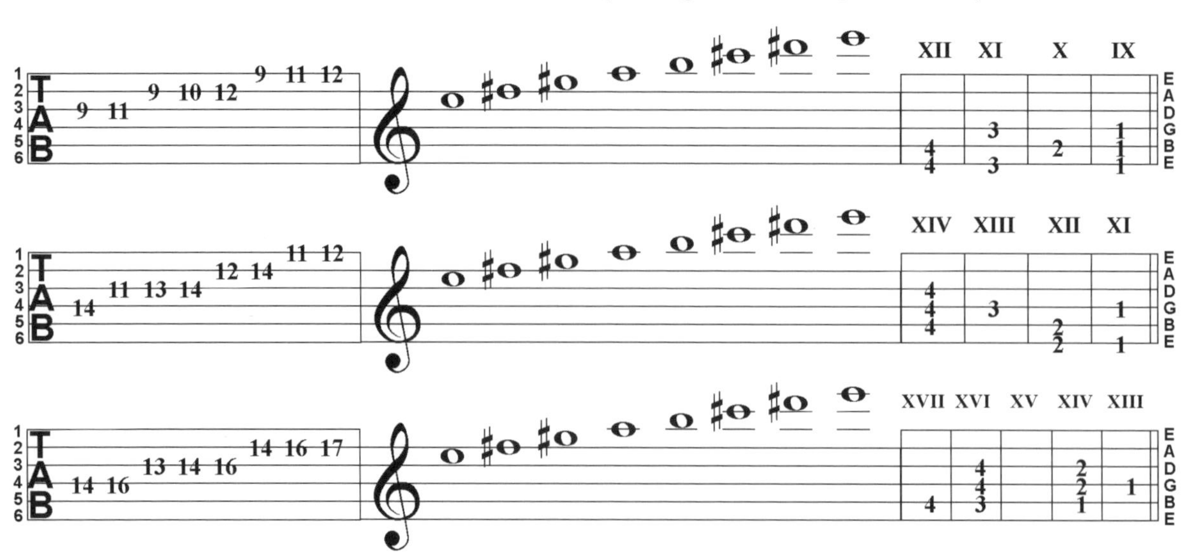

CD track 7 – Rhythm 'n' Blues

♫ = ♩³♪

| 4/4 A7 | A7 | A7 | F7. E7. | D7 | D7 | E7 | E7 ||

Grade 3 level performance	
Suggested scale:	A blues – 2 octaves, 1 position
Best bends:	Upper octave – 4th(D) to 5th(E), ♭7th(G) to octave(A)

Grade 4 level performance	
Suggested scale:	A blues – 2 octaves, 2 positions
Best bends:	2nd position, upper octave – ♭3rd(C) to 4th(D)

Grade 5 level performance	
Suggested scale:	A blues – 1 octave, 5 positions

A blues scale – 2 octaves (2 fingerboard positions)

A	C	D	E♭	E	G	A
1	♭3	4	♭5	5	♭7	8

A blues scale – 1 octave (5 fingerboard positions)

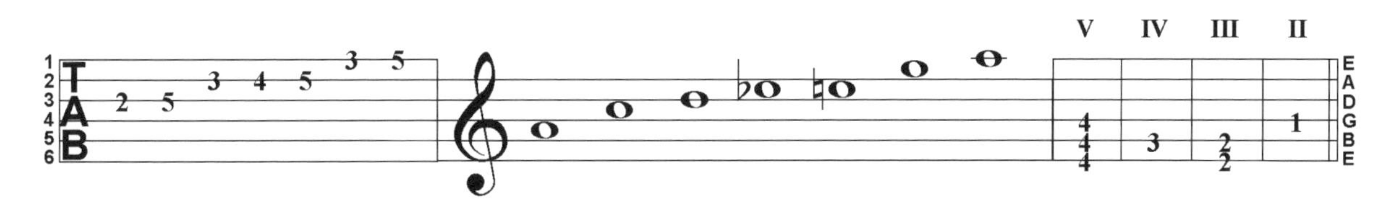

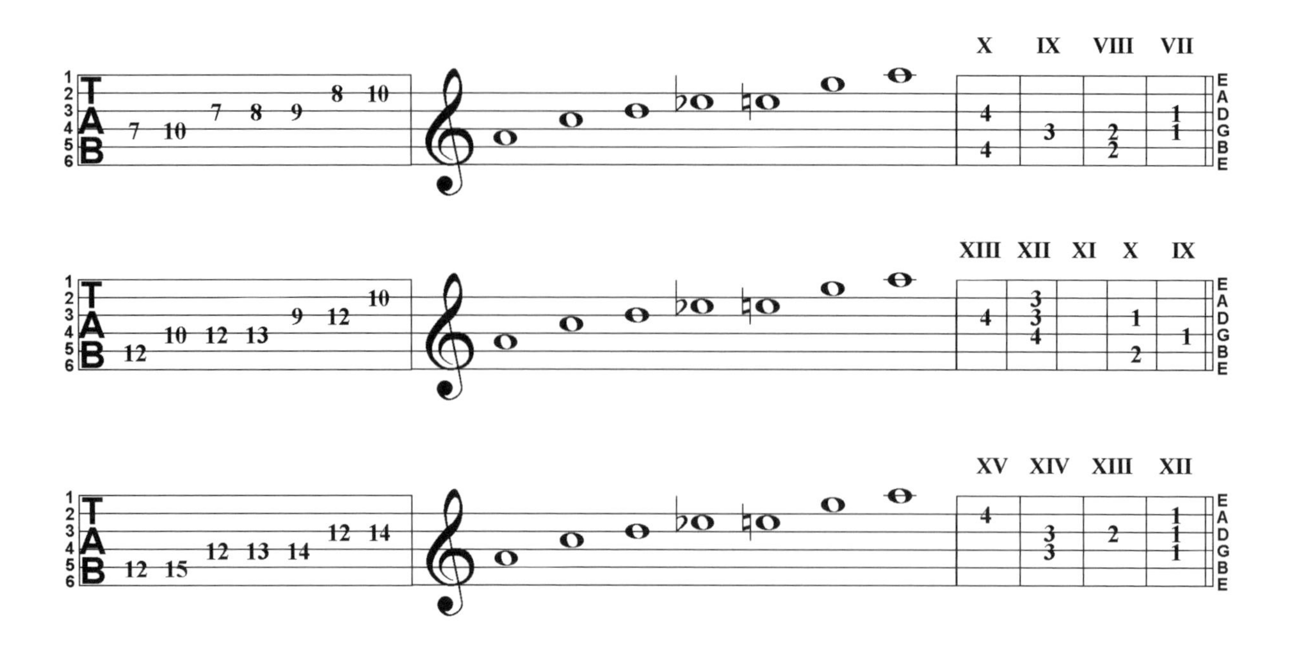

CD track 8 – Motown Groove

| 4/4 F7 | F7 | A♭ | B♭7 | F7 | F7 | B♭7 | C7 ||

Grade 3 level performance	
Suggested scale:	F blues – 2 octaves, 1 position
Best bends:	Upper octave – 4th(B♭) to 5th(C), ♭7th(E♭) to octave(F)

Grade 4 level performance	
Suggested scale:	F blues – 2 octaves, 2 positions
Best bends:	2nd shape, upper octave – ♭3rd(A♭) to 4th(B♭)

Grade 5 level performance	
Suggested scale:	F blues – 1 octave, 5 positions

To learn the F blues scales refer to the blues scale shapes shown on page 23. These can be transposed to F blues by starting each shape on an F rather than an A. (Some of the scale shapes can be transposed an octave to avoid awkward fingerboard positions.)

CD track 9 – Blues Swing

♫ = ♩³♪

| 4/4 B♭7 | E♭7 | B♭7 | B♭7 | E♭7 | E♭7 | G♭7 | F7 ||

Grade 3 level performance	
Suggested scale:	B♭ blues – 2 octaves, 1 position
Best bends:	Upper octave – 4th(E♭) to 5th(F), ♭7th(A♭) to octave(B♭)

Grade 4 level performance	
Suggested scale:	B♭ blues – 2 octaves, 2 positions
Best bends:	2nd shape, upper octave – ♭3rd(D♭) to 4th(E♭)

Grade 5 level performance	
Suggested scale:	B♭ blues – 1 octave, 5 positions

To learn the B♭ blues scales refer to the blues scale shapes shown on pages 23 and 24. These can be transposed to B♭ blues by playing one fret higher than illustrated.

CD track 10 – Disco Funk

| 4/4 Dmaj7 | D6 | Bm | Bm7 | Em7 | G6 | Asus4 | A7 ||

Grade 3 level performance	
Suggested scale:	D major – 2 octaves, 1 position

Grade 4 level performance	
Suggested scale:	D major – 2 octaves, 2 positions
Best bends:	Upper octaves – 2nd(E) to 3rd(F#), 4th(G) to 5th(A), 5th(A) to 6th(B), 6th(B) to 7th(C#)

Grade 5 level performance	
Suggested scale:	D major – 1 octave, 3 positions

To learn the D major scales refer to the E major scale shapes shown on page 22. These can be transposed to D major by playing two frets lower than illustrated.

CD track 11 – Latin Groove

| 4/4 Bm | F#7 | F#7 | Bm | Bm | G7.F#7. | G7.F#7. | Bm.F#7. ||

Grade 5 level performance	
Suggested scale:	B harmonic minor – 2 octaves, 1 position
Best bends:	Upper octave – 4th(E) to 5th(F#)

B harmonic minor scale – 2 octaves

B	C#	D	E	F#	G	A#	B
1	2	♭3	4	5	♭6	7	8

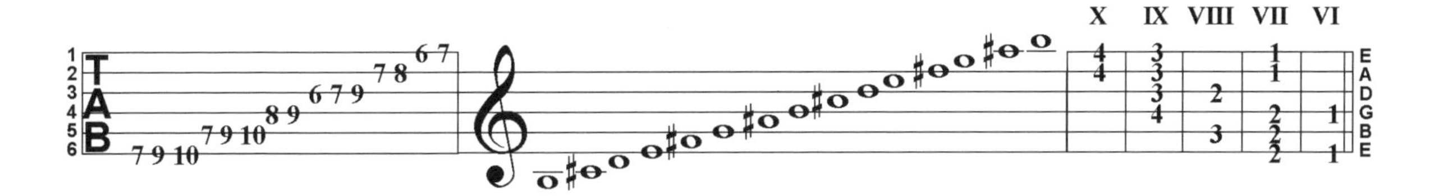

Where next?

Once you've played through all the tracks using the suggested scales, it's worth having a look at the arpeggio shapes shown on the following pages. Try to use some of these shapes to help break away from using only the basic key scales. Arpeggios are a good way of making your improvisation more melodic and creative. Give them a try...

Arpeggio shapes

The most useful arpeggios for Intermediate level players are shown below. To enable easy comparison between arpeggios all are illustrated starting on C. However, as all the patterns are transpositional, it is quite easy to learn arpeggios other than C. You only need to replicate the fingering starting on a different note. For example, to play the B major arpeggio simply play the C major arpeggio pattern starting one fret lower on B.

C major arpeggio – 2 octaves

C E G C
1 3 5 8

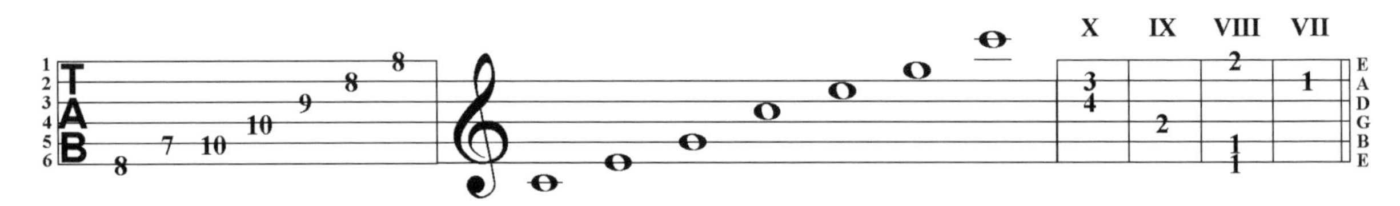

C major 7th arpeggio – 2 octaves

C E G B C
1 3 5 7 8

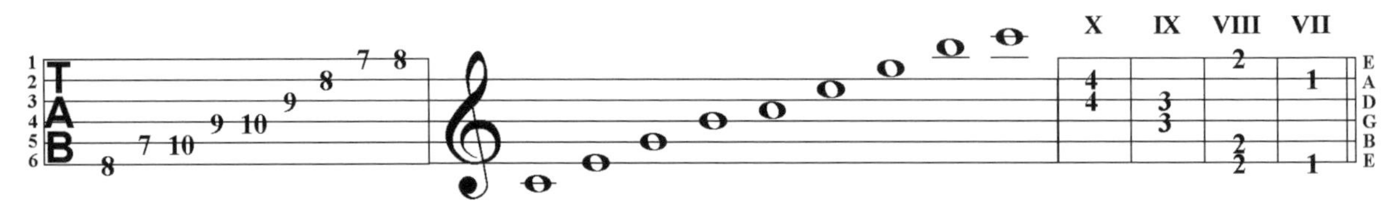

C major 7th arpeggio – 1 octave (2 fingerboard positions)

C E G B C
1 3 5 7 8

C dominant 7th arpeggio – 2 octaves

C E G B♭ C

1 3 5 ♭7 8

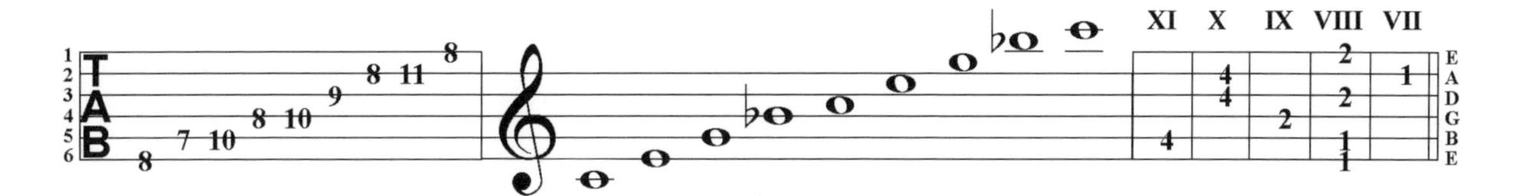

C dominant 7th arpeggio – 1 octave (2 fingerboard positions)

C E G B♭ C

1 3 5 ♭7 8

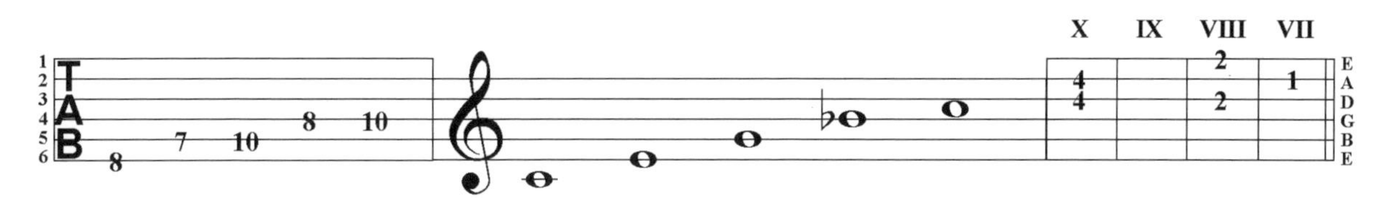

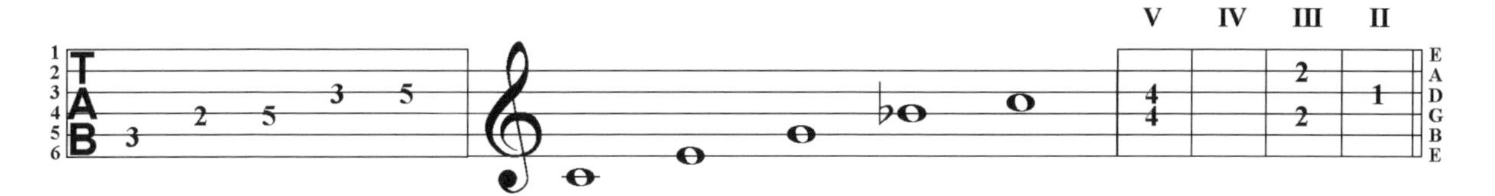

C minor arpeggio – 2 octaves

C E♭ G C

1 ♭3 5 8

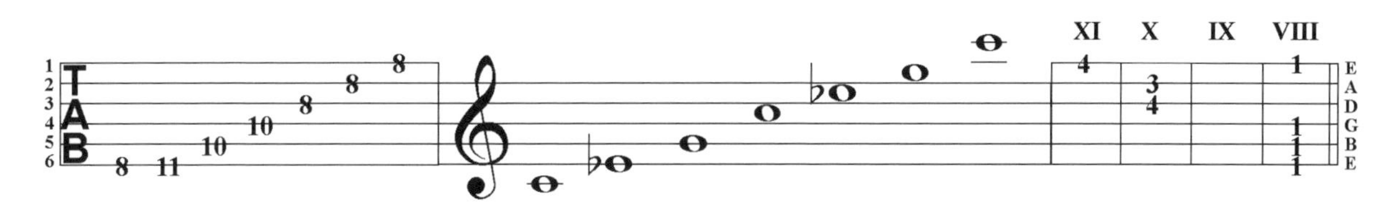

C minor 7th arpeggio – 2 octaves

C E♭ G B♭ C

1 ♭3 5 ♭7 8

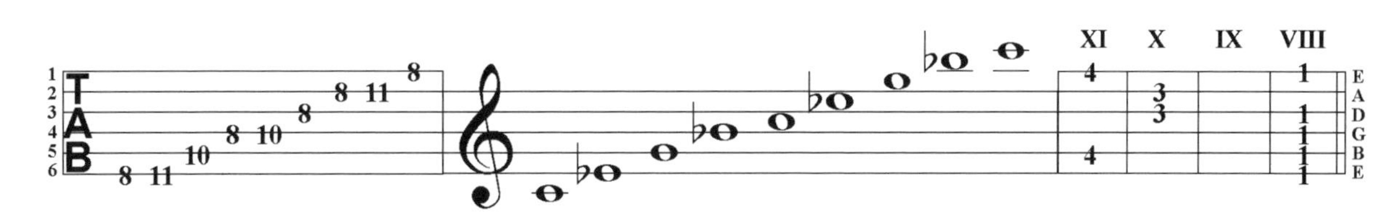

C minor 7th arpeggio – 1 octave (2 fingerboard positions)

C Eb G Bb C

1 b3 5 b7 8

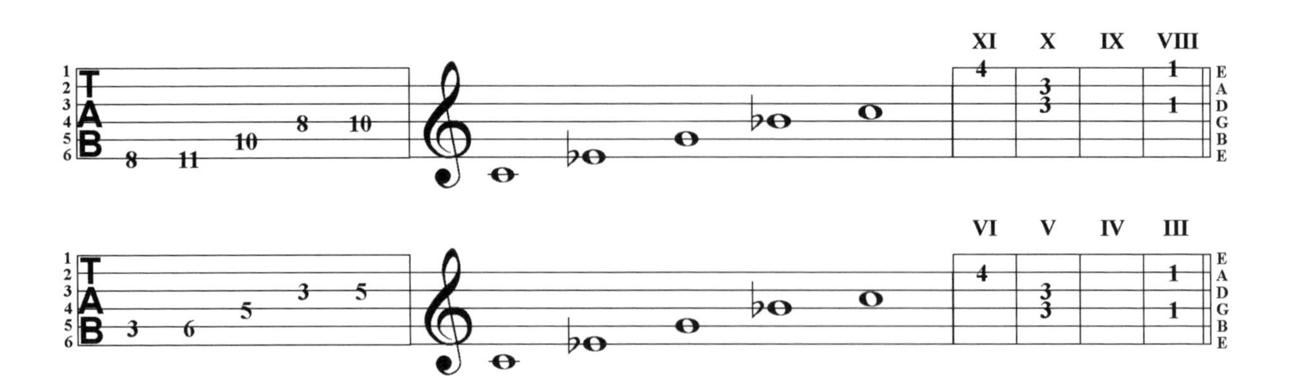

C sus 4 arpeggio – 1 octave (2 fingerboard positions)

C F G C

1 4 5 8

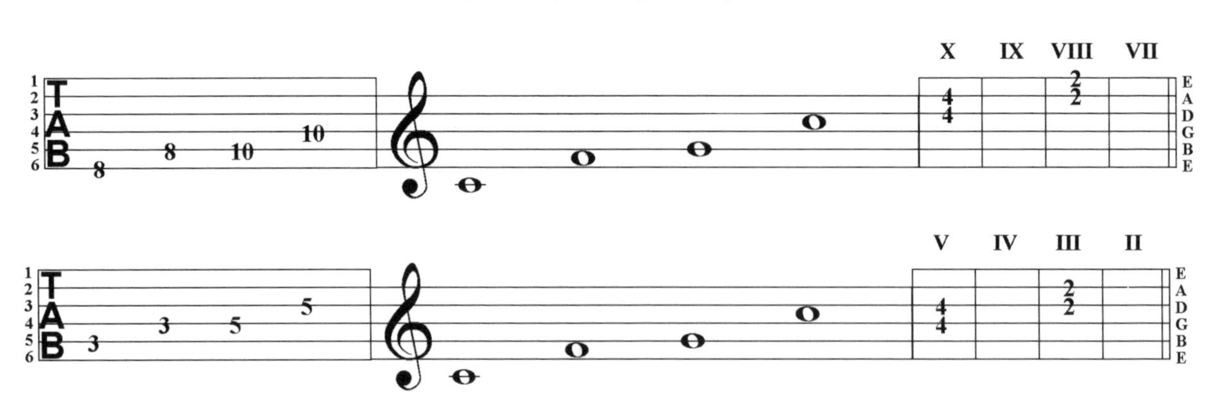

C major 6th arpeggio – 1 octave (2 fingerboard positions)

C E G A C

1 3 5 6 8

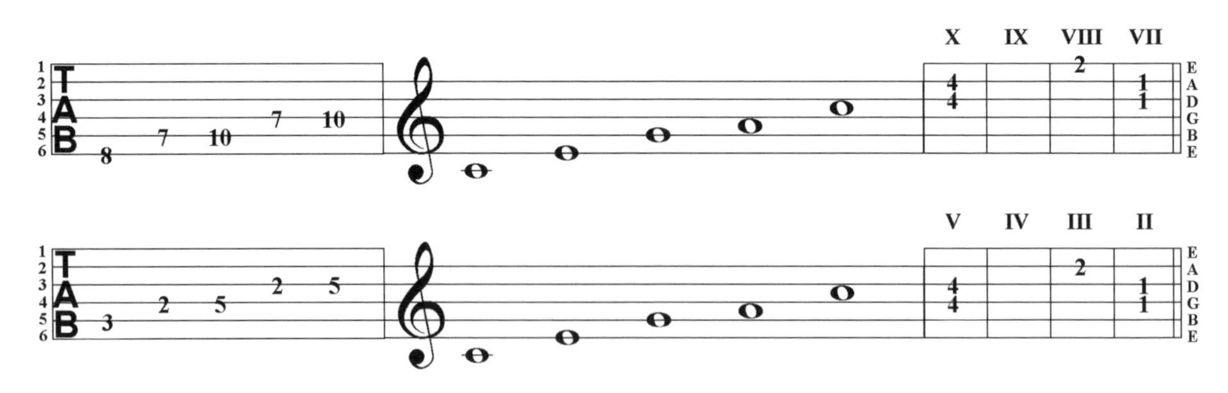

Make the grade

By working through all the material in this book you will have covered most of the requirements of the Scales and Lead Guitar sections of the Registry of Guitar Tutors electric guitar examination syllabus – Grades Three to Five.

To make sure that you develop your guitar playing in a structured and comprehensive way, you should study the other sections of the examination syllabus.

These are:

- Chords
- Rhythm Playing
- Musical Knowledge
- Aural Awareness

Studying all these topics will greatly help you improve as a guitar player. The books shown overleaf are specifically designed to help you develop your guitar playing in these areas.

You can order them from your local book store or directly from the Registry.

Further study

Electric Guitar Playing

(Grade Five) by Tony Skinner

Can you make the grade? Find out by reading this book!

If you learn to play all the things contained within this book you will be able to gain an internationally recognised qualification in electric guitar playing. It covers all the areas of guitar playing and musical knowledge that you need to pass your RGT Grade Five examination.

Even if you're not interested in exams, the handbook will help you to become a much improved guitarist and fully rounded musician.

Rhythm Guitar Playing

(Book Two) by Chaz Hart

Is your rhythm playing as good as your lead? If not, this is the book for you!

It contains over 30 chord sequences for you to practise, and gives plenty of advice and tips on how to improve your rhythm playing.

All the chords required for the Grade Three, Four and Five examinations are fully covered in this book.

You can order these books from your local book store or from www.BooksForGuitar.com

Registry Mews, 11-13 Wilton Road, Bexhill, Sussex, TN40 1HY, United Kingdom.
Tel: 01424 222222 Fax: 01424 213221
Website: www.RegistryOfGuitarTutors.com